Living Prayer

Learning to Pray in Daily Life

— JOHN DAVEY —

Sacristy
Press

Sacristy Press
PO Box 612, Durham, DH1 9HT

www.sacristy.co.uk

First published in 2017 by Sacristy Press, Durham

Copyright © John Davey 2017
The moral rights of the author have been asserted

All rights reserved, no part of this publication may be reproduced
or transmitted in any form or by any means, electronic,
mechanical photocopying, documentary, film or in any other
format without prior written permission of the publisher.

Scripture quotations are drawn from THE HOLY BIBLE, NEW
INTERNATIONAL VERSION®, NIV®. Copyright © 1973, 1978, 1984,
2011 by Biblica, Inc.® Used by permission. All rights reserved worldwide.

Copyright material is included from *Common Worship:
Services and Prayers for the Church of England.*
Copyright © The Archbishops' Council 2000.

Extracts from The Book of Common Prayer, the rights in
which are vested in the Crown, are reproduced by permission
of the Crown's patentee, Cambridge University Press.

Every reasonable effort has been made to trace the copyright holders
of material reproduced in this book, but if any have been inadvertently
overlooked the publisher would be glad to hear from them.

Sacristy Limited, registered in England & Wales, number 7565667

British Library Cataloguing-in-Publication Data
A catalogue record for the book is available from the British Library

ISBN 978-1-910519-61-5

To all who have sought to understand the meaning of life, and the relevance of their being in the vastness of a universe that stretches beyond the comprehension of man.

Preface

In my forty years of pastoral ministry I have been asked on countless occasions "Where is God when you need him most?" and "Why are prayers left unanswered?" It is hard to provide a convincing answer to those who feel utterly abandoned at their time of greatest need. For those who are called upon to make intercession for others, it is especially challenging. Enlightenment came when, in prayer, I gazed at the stained-glass figure of the crucified Christ in the East Window of my church and saw suffering beyond human endurance. The words of the Eucharistic prayer echoed in my mind: "I have done this for you. Do this for me." How blind I had been. God had answered the prayers of all humanity and for all time on the cross.

It was the key that unlocked the door of understanding. Christ's hands were my hands; his love was mine to share; his pain was mine to bear. Prayer was not about asking God to do something for us, but the remembrance that we must do something for him, and be his body and his presence in the gifts of our love and service to others in his name.

Prayer is the movement of the heart, mind, and will to that inner voice which calls us to the acknowledgement of God's presence. The prayers in this book are by way of an introduction to the practice of daily prayer, a practice that can transform and enrich our life and the lives of those around us as we grow in grace.

For those who, for one reason or another, do not attend a regular act of worship, this discipline will be of particular value.

Contents

Preface iv

The Prayer that Jesus Taught Us 1
First Steps 7
Prayer, The Breath of Our Being 11
Morning Prayers 13
Evening Prayers 19
Night Prayers 23
Praying with the Psalter 31
Living the Liturgy 47

Epilogue 51

The Prayer that Jesus Taught Us

The most familiar prayer of all for Christians is the prayer which Jesus himself taught us:

> One day Jesus was praying in a certain place. When he finished, one of his disciples said to him, "Lord, teach us to pray, just as John taught his disciples."
> He said to them, "When you pray, say:
> 'Father,
> hallowed be your name,
> your kingdom come.
> Give us each day our daily bread.
> Forgive us our sins,
> for we also forgive everyone who sins against us.
> And lead us not into temptation.'"
>
> *Luke 11:1–4*

In this prayer we are asking God to make his world our world, his will our will. The daily bread spoken of is none other than the bread of life. Jesus said to his disciples:

> "Very truly I tell you, it is not Moses who has given you the bread from heaven, but it is my Father who gives you the true bread from heaven. For the bread of God is the bread that comes down from heaven and gives life to the world."
>
> "Sir," they said, "always give us this bread."
>
> Then Jesus declared, "I am the bread of life. Whoever comes to me will never go hungry, and whoever believes in me will never be thirsty."
>
> ***John 6:32–35***

The forgiveness of sins is an expression of the divine love that we are called upon to share with others. Lastly, we ask for strength to turn away from temptation and to follow the way of the Lord.

Addressing God in prayer, Jesus uses the word Abba, as would a child to a father, an intimate term that speaks of trust, obedience, and love. This relationship between Father and Son is exemplified in St Luke's account of Christ's baptism, as is the relationship between prayer and presence.

> When all the people were being baptized, Jesus was baptized too. And as he was praying, heaven was opened and the Holy Spirit descended on him in bodily form like a dove. And a voice came from heaven: "You are my Son, whom I love; with you I am well pleased."
>
> ***Luke 3:21–22***

St Mark records in his gospel two occasions that illustrate how prayer is the source of the power which underpinned Christ's ministry of teaching and healing. The first is at the beginning of his Galilean ministry:

> Very early in the morning, while it was still dark, Jesus got up, left the house and went off to a solitary place, where he prayed. Simon and his companions went to look for him, and when they found him, they exclaimed: "Everyone is looking for you!"
>
> ***Mark 1:35–37***

And Jesus, returning from the mount of transfiguration, was met by a bewildered father who said:

> "Teacher, I brought you my son, who is possessed by a spirit that has robbed him of speech. Whenever it seizes him, it throws him to the ground. He foams at the mouth, gnashes his teeth and becomes rigid. I asked your disciples to drive out the spirit, but they could not."
>
> After Jesus had gone indoors, his disciples asked him privately, "Why couldn't we drive it out?"
>
> He replied, "This kind can come out only by prayer."
>
> ***Mark 9:17–18, 28–29***

The Gospel of John takes us further in our understanding of the life-giving power of prayer. Jesus at the grave of Lazarus thanks the Father for a life restored.

> So they took away the stone. Then Jesus looked up and said, "Father, I thank you that you have heard me. I knew that you always hear me, but I said this for the benefit of the people standing here, that they may believe that you sent me."
>
> ***John 11:41–42***

THE PRAYER THAT JESUS TAUGHT US

At the last supper Jesus said to his disciples:

> Believe me when I say that I am in the Father and the Father is in me; or at least believe on the evidence of the works themselves. Very truly I tell you, whoever believes in me will do the works I have been doing, and they will do even greater things than these, because I am going to the Father. And I will do whatever you ask in my name, so that the Father may be glorified in the Son. You may ask me for anything in my name, and I will do it.
>
> ***John 14:11–14***

> If you remain in me and my words remain in you, ask whatever you wish, and it will be done for you. This is to my Father's glory, that you bear much fruit, showing yourselves to be my disciples.
>
> As the Father has loved me, so have I loved you. Now remain in my love.
>
> ***John 15:7–9***

Prayer, to be answered, must come from an abiding faith in the Lord Jesus and for the words of his teaching to penetrate to the very core of our being. This is *Living Prayer*.

First Steps

When we call upon the name of the Lord, he hears our voice. It is not that he has come to join us from beyond the clouds or from outer space. He is ever-present. But we need to be reminded of this fact in order to experience the fact. The presence of God in human form is an awesome proposition. No wonder his disciples found it difficult to believe that Jesus and the Father were one, and that no one has seen the Father except through him. It is even more difficult to accept the blinding truth revealed to St Paul on the Damascus Road: the secret, as he wrote in his letters to the early Church, that Christ Jesus dwells in us through the power and grace of the promised Comforter, the Holy Spirit.

Often, an external stimulus helps to bring together the within-ness and the other-ness of our being. A lighted candle can remind us of his presence. So, too, can our body posture. Kneeling in prayer has largely gone out of fashion and is not really necessary to indicate supplication. More telling is the simple act of opening one's palms in a gesture of reception. In Holy Communion we receive bread and wine, symbols of Christ's presence, in a like manner, and in partaking of the sacrament we become the sacrament. Likewise, as we open our hearts and minds to the inner presence of God in prayer, we become at one with him, and he with us. We are taught in our catechism that a sacrament is the outward and visible sign of an inward and spiritual grace. As we respond to God's will, revealed to us in prayer, we are enabled to become a living testament to his presence, a sign to the world of his grace. One can create a point of stillness in the most unlikely of places: a commuter train or bus, waiting for an appointment at the doctor's surgery or at the dentist, even in a queue at the supermarket checkout. Nowhere are we absent from the presence of God, for he is ever with us.

Ideally, however, one should have a special place, a quiet spot to which one can retreat from the distractions of the world around us. The time set aside for prayer need not be long; it is the direction of the mind and will to the mind and will of God through the prompting of the Holy Spirit that is important.

Setting aside a moment of time to reflect on the Name of Jesus takes us right back to Our Lord's own habit of seeking out a place of quietude to commune with the Father.

To his disciples, Jesus said:

> But when you pray, go into your room, close the door and pray to your Father, who is unseen. Then your Father, who sees what is done in secret, will reward you. And when you pray, do not keep on babbling like pagans, for they think they will be heard because of their many words. Do not be like them, for your Father knows what you need before you ask him.
>
> ***Matthew 6:6-8***

A "room by yourself" is figurative. It is your private space. Remember, the Spirit of God is not a mighty clap of thunder; he is the still, small voice that comes from within the stillness of our being. In this moment of stillness, say quietly to yourself:

> The Lord is here—His Spirit is with us.

> No one can say, "Jesus is Lord," except by the Holy Spirit.
>
> ***1 Corinthians 12:3***

Think of the magnitude and breadth of what we are saying. It is the doorway through which Jesus will enter into our lives.

> Here I am! I stand at the door and knock. If anyone hears my voice and opens the door, I will come in and eat with that person, and they with me.
>
> ***Revelation 3:20***

Jesus, dwelling with us, being part of our life, sharing our home, and our every emotion, be it joy or sorrow, is a life-changing experience for us and for the world around us. A very personal thank-you prayer I say when I greet the day is:

> Thank you, Mary, for bringing Our Saviour into the world, and thank you, Jesus, for being at one with us in our humanity.

Prayer, The Breath of Our Being

In your quiet place recite this prayer as though it were the breath of your being:

> Lord Jesus, Son of the Living God, have mercy on me, a sinner.

Draw in breath slowly at the words *Lord Jesus, Son of the Living God*, expelling with the words *have mercy on me, a sinner*.

As you practice this prayer, think of the taking in of breath as inviting Jesus into your life and receiving his loving forgiveness, and the expelling of breath as letting go of all that is unworthy of his presence. An ancillary effect of this prayer is to bring a sense of calm at times of stress and crisis by combining prayer with controlled breathing, whereby it becomes a vehicle of healing grace.

Morning Prayers

Beginning the day with prayer can be compared to having your mobile phone fully charged and being ready for any emergency. The morning may not be the best of times to set aside a moment of stillness with a busy day ahead of you, but, with practice, prayer can become part of your daily routine, like brushing your teeth. Prayer does not have to be either complicated or lengthy. Begin by saying the prayer that Jesus taught us:

> Our Father in heaven,
> Hallowed be your name,
> Your Kingdom come,
> Your will be done,
> On earth as in heaven.
> Give us today our daily bread.
> Forgive us our sins
> As we forgive those who sin against us.
> Lead us not into temptation
> But deliver us from evil. Amen.

Then:

> Help me, Lord, to become the person you want me to be, and direct what I ought to do in your name this day. Amen.

Words of assurance

> Grant me, merciful Father, pardon and peace,
> That I may be cleansed from all my sins,
> And serve you with a quiet mind this day
> And every day, through Jesus
>   Christ Our Lord. Amen.

Prayers of commendation

> Into your hands, O Lord, I commend myself, and all who are dear to me. Be with me today in my going out and my coming in. Strengthen me for my daily work and grant that, filled with your Holy Spirit, I may be worthy of your love and accomplish those things you have called me to do in your name, through Jesus Christ Our Lord. Amen.

Accomplishing the things God has called us to do *in his name* is a sign of God's grace and the fulfilment of God's promise of the coming of his Kingdom. The fruits of the Holy Spirit are, as St Paul frequently reminds us, Love, Joy, Peace, Patience, Goodness, Fidelity, Kindness, Gentleness, and Self-Control. The signs of God's abiding love and compassion should be reflected in what we do and say and in our loving concern for others.

> Lord, may your blessing rest upon those for whom I ought to pray, watch over the young, support the aged, relieve those in pain or sickness, comfort the sorrowful, succour the dying, and let your peace be with them now and ever more. Amen.

> Father, be my strength today in every time and need. Be my guide through all the dark places and be my guard against all that threatens my tranquillity, that I may have joy in my heart in the assurance of your peace and presence; through Jesus Christ your Son. Amen.

You may wish to include one of the following prayers:

Prayer of St Francis

Lord, make me an instrument of your peace,
Where there is hatred, let me sow love;
Where there is injury, pardon,
Where there is discord, union,
Where there is doubt, faith,
Where there is despair, hope,
Where there is darkness, light,
Where there is sadness, joy,
For your mercy and truth's sake. Amen.

Prayer of St Richard

Thank you, Lord Jesus,
For all the blessings you have won for me,
For all the pains and insults you have born for me.
Most merciful redeemer, friend and brother,
May I know you more clearly, love you more dearly,
And follow you more nearly this
   day and always. Amen.

Prayer of St Benedict

Gracious and Holy Father,
Give me:
Intellect to understand you;
Reason to discern you;
Diligence to seek you;
Wisdom to find you;
A spirit to know you;
A heart to meditate upon you;
Ears to hear you;
Eyes to see you;
A tongue to proclaim you;
A way of life pleasing to you;
Patience to wait for you;
Perseverance to look for you. Amen.

Prayer of St Ignatius

Teach me, good Lord, to serve you as you deserve,
To give and not to count the cost,
To fight and not to heed the words,
To toil and not to look for rest,
To labour and not to ask for any reward,
Save that of knowing that I do your will.

Evening Prayers

Evening is a time to reflect on the events of the day and to share with Jesus the joys and sorrows which it has brought. As with our morning prayer, begin with the prayer that Jesus taught us:

> Our Father . . .

Follow this with a prayer of contrition.

> Father, I have left undone things I should have done and have done things I should not have done. For your Son Our Lord Jesus Christ's sake, forgive me and grant that, in the assurance of your loving grace, I may lead a new life to the glory of His Holy Name. Amen.

A thank-you prayer

For your humble birth in Bethlehem,
For revealing the presence of God in your humanity,
For your obedience to the divine will of your Father,
For the simplicity of your teaching,
For your loving compassion,
For the forgiveness of our sins,
For your suffering on the cross,
For the triumph of the resurrection,
And the promise of new life in the Spirit,
Thank you, Lord Jesus. Amen.

Praying for others

Loving Lord, may all who strive to bring health and well-being to the sick in mind or body, the hungry, the poor, and the disadvantaged, be strengthened by the power of the Holy Spirit to continue the work you have begun in Christ Jesus your Son, especially ... [here we might name specific charities and organisations that we support].

Linking our prayers with charitable giving is a practical response to Our Lord's words:

> For I was hungry and you gave me nothing to eat, I was thirsty and you gave me nothing to drink, I was a stranger and you did not invite me in, I needed clothes and you did not clothe me, I was sick and in prison and you did not look after me.
>
> They also will answer, "Lord, when did we see you hungry or thirsty or a stranger or needing clothes or sick or in prison, and did not help you?"
>
> He will reply, "Truly I tell you, whatever you did not do for one of the least of these, you did not do for me."
>
> ***Matthew 25:42–45***

Save me, Lord, from thinking only of my own needs and desires; and help me to remember that it is more blessed to give than to receive. Amen.

Father, grant me the will to think of others and their needs before my own, mindful that all I possess and all that I am is held in trust for you and for the service of others in your name. Amen.

Night Prayers

At the end of a busy day, when you are tired and ready for bed, night prayers might be the very last thing on your mind, but the minute or so you spend in prayer before going to sleep has a deeply significant part to play in Living Prayer. The last service of the day in religious communities is compline, and this has been so for some fifteen hundred years. Compline is derived from the Latin *completorium*, the completion of the working day. It is a service of quietness and reflection.

Beginning with an invocation of God's blessing, it is followed by prayers of penitence, a psalm, a reading from scripture, responsory prayers placing oneself into the hands of God, the Nunc Dimittis, the Collect of the day, intercessions and thanksgiving, and ends with The Lord's Prayer.

Forgiveness lies at the heart of Christ's ministry and is an essential part of his teaching. It is the gateway to the healing process, as illustrated in the following passage from St Luke's Gospel.

> Some men came carrying a paralyzed man on a mat and tried to take him into the house to lay him before Jesus. When they could not find a way to do this because of the crowd, they went up on the roof and lowered him on his mat through the tiles into the middle of the crowd, right in front of Jesus.
>
> When Jesus saw their faith, he said, "Friend, your sins are forgiven."
>
> The Pharisees and the teachers of the law began thinking to themselves, "Who is this fellow who speaks blasphemy? Who can forgive sins but God alone?"
>
> Jesus knew what they were thinking and asked, "Why are you thinking these things in your hearts? Which is easier: to say, 'Your sins are forgiven,' or to say, 'Get up and walk'? But I want you to know that the Son of Man has authority on earth to forgive sins." So he said to the paralyzed man, "I tell you, get up, take your mat and go home." Immediately he stood up in front of them, took what he had been lying on and went home praising God. Everyone was amazed and gave praise to God. They were filled with awe and said, "We have seen remarkable things today."
>
> *Luke 5:18–26*

Forgiveness is the ultimate sign of the unconditional love of God.

A prayer of penitence

Forgive, Lord, the things I have done this day that I should not have done, and the things I did not do which I should have done, and help me, by the power and grace of the Holy Spirit, to become the person you want me to be.

Placing oneself into the hands of God

Thank you, Lord, for all the blessings of this day. Grant me the assurance of your peace, and take me, and all whom I love, into your care this night; for Jesus Christ's sake. Amen.

O Lord, support us all the day long,
until the shadows lengthen, and the evening comes,
and the busy world is hushed,
and the fever of life is over,
and our work is done.
Then in your mercy
grant us a safe lodging and a holy rest,
and peace at the last. Amen.

John Henry Newman

Almighty God, at whose command we go forth
to our work by day and take our rest at night,
grant me the precious gift of sleep, that I may
awake refreshed and renewed for your service,
through Jesus Christ Our Lord. Amen.

Rest and renewal are key factors in making our night prayers an important staging post in our journey of faith, a journey from darkness to light.

A new day and new life

The sacrificial death of Christ on the cross for the sins of the world, and the dawn of new life for humankind in the triumph of the resurrection, is echoed in our petition for forgiveness and resolution to try, with God's help, to be a better person.

A compline prayer

O Lord Jesus Christ, Son of the living God, who at this evening hour didst rest in the sepulchre, and didst thereby sanctify the grave to be a bed of hope to thy people: Make us so to abound in sorrow for our sins, which were the cause of thy passion, that when our bodies lie in the dust, our souls may live with thee; who livest and reignest with the Father and the Holy Ghost, one God, world without end. Amen.

Common Worship

There is no going back, no dwelling upon the past. On Easter Day, the day of Resurrection, the words of the Psalmist ring out in Christendom:

> This is the day which the Lord hath made: we will rejoice and be glad in it.
> **_Book of Common Prayer, Psalm 118:24_**

The recorded life of Jesus in the gospels spans a period, apart from the birth narratives, of about three years, and, knowing the inevitability of his fate, there is a sense of urgency about Christ's ministry of teaching and healing. The Kingdom of God has come: it is here, it is now, it is the central message. Each and every day is a "Kingdom" day. The Sermon on the Mount (Matthew 5–6) provides us with an ethical framework on which to base our interaction with the world around us, and, as the extract below shows, if we get it wrong, we can put the past behind us and start again. Night prayer helps us to do this.

> Therefore I tell you, do not worry about your life, what you will eat or drink; or about your body, what you will wear. Is not life more than food, and the body more than clothes? Look at the birds of the air; they do not sow or reap or store away in barns, and yet your heavenly Father feeds them. Are you not much more valuable than they? Can any one of you by worrying add a single hour to your life?

And why do you worry about clothes? See how the flowers of the field grow. They do not labor or spin. Yet I tell you that not even Solomon in all his splendor was dressed like one of these. If that is how God clothes the grass of the field, which is here today and tomorrow is thrown into the fire, will he not much more clothe you—you of little faith? So do not worry, saying, "What shall we eat?" or "What shall we drink?" or "What shall we wear?" For the pagans run after all these things, and your heavenly Father knows that you need them. But seek first his kingdom and his righteousness, and all these things will be given to you as well. Therefore do not worry about tomorrow, for tomorrow will worry about itself. Each day has enough trouble of its own.

Matthew 6:25–34

Living Prayer is the fulfilment of promise that, by the grace and power of the Holy Spirit, we will become living witnesses to the presence of the Risen Christ.

Praying with the Psalter

Written over a long period of time, the psalms of David became the hymn book of the Temple and form the bedrock of daily worship to this day. In the psalms, every mood and condition of life is brought before God. Although the psalms express every kind of feeling, their note of joy predominates.

In Mark's account of the crucifixion, Our Lord, at the ninth hour, cried out with a loud voice, "My God, my God, why hast thou forsaken me?" At the moment of dying, he recalled the words of Psalm 22, which he had come to fulfil. We might think that these opening words of the psalm are a cry of despair, but the psalm is one of victory. When Jesus came to bring comfort to his disciples after the resurrection, he said to them:

> This is what I told you while I was still with you: Everything must be fulfilled that is written about me in the Law of Moses, the Prophets and the Psalms.
>
> ***Luke 24:44***

The concluding verses of Psalm 22 are testimony to the divine grace of God and the fulfilment of his promise of salvation.

Psalm 22:26–31

> The poor will eat and be satisfied;
> those who seek the Lord will praise him—
> may your hearts live forever!
> All the ends of the earth
> will remember and turn to the Lord,
> and all the families of the nations
> will bow down before him,
> for dominion belongs to the Lord
> and he rules over the nations.
> All the rich of the earth will feast and worship;
> all who go down to the dust will kneel before him—
> those who cannot keep themselves alive.
> Posterity will serve him;
> future generations will be told about the Lord.
> They will proclaim his righteousness,
> declaring to a people yet unborn:
> He has done it!

Psalm 15

Lord, who may dwell in your sacred tent?
Who may live on your holy mountain?
The one whose walk is blameless,
who does what is righteous,
who speaks the truth from their heart;
whose tongue utters no slander,
who does no wrong to a neighbour,
and casts no slur on others;
who despises a vile person
but honours those who fear the Lord;
who keeps an oath even when it hurts,
and does not change their mind;
who lends money to the poor without interest;
who does not accept a bribe against the innocent.
Whoever does these things
will never be shaken.

Psalm 23

The Lord is my shepherd, I lack nothing.
He makes me lie down in green pastures,
he leads me beside quiet waters,
he refreshes my soul.
He guides me along the right paths
for his name's sake.
Even though I walk
through the darkest valley,
I will fear no evil,
for you are with me;
your rod and your staff,
they comfort me.
You prepare a table before me
in the presence of my enemies.
You anoint my head with oil;
my cup overflows.
Surely your goodness and love will follow me
all the days of my life,
and I will dwell in the house of the Lord
forever.

Psalm 27

The Lord is my light and my salvation—
whom shall I fear?
The Lord is the stronghold of my life—
of whom shall I be afraid?
When the wicked advance against me
to devour me,
it is my enemies and my foes
who will stumble and fall.
Though an army besiege me,
my heart will not fear;
though war break out against me,
even then I will be confident.
One thing I ask from the Lord,
this only do I seek:
that I may dwell in the house of the Lord
all the days of my life,
to gaze on the beauty of the Lord
and to seek him in his temple.
For in the day of trouble
he will keep me safe in his dwelling;
he will hide me in the shelter of his sacred tent
and set me high upon a rock.
Then my head will be exalted
above the enemies who surround me;
at his sacred tent I will sacrifice with shouts of joy;
I will sing and make music to the Lord.
Hear my voice when I call, Lord;

be merciful to me and answer me.
My heart says of you, "Seek his face!"
Your face, Lord, I will seek.
Do not hide your face from me,
do not turn your servant away in anger;
you have been my helper.
Do not reject me or forsake me,
God my Savior.
Though my father and mother forsake me,
the Lord will receive me.
Teach me your way, Lord;
lead me in a straight path
because of my oppressors.
Do not turn me over to the desire of my foes,
for false witnesses rise up against me,
spouting malicious accusations.
I remain confident of this:
I will see the goodness of the Lord
in the land of the living.
Wait for the Lord;
be strong and take heart
and wait for the Lord.

Psalm 46

God is our refuge and strength,
an ever-present help in trouble.
Therefore we will not fear, though the earth give way
and the mountains fall into the heart of the sea,
though its waters roar and foam
and the mountains quake with their surging.
There is a river whose streams make
   glad the city of God,
the holy place where the Most High dwells.
God is within her, she will not fall;
God will help her at break of day.
Nations are in uproar, kingdoms fall;
he lifts his voice, the earth melts.
The Lord Almighty is with us;
the God of Jacob is our fortress.
Come and see what the Lord has done,
the desolations he has brought on the earth.
He makes wars cease
to the ends of the earth.
He breaks the bow and shatters the spear;
he burns the shields with fire.
He says, "Be still, and know that I am God;
I will be exalted among the nations,
I will be exalted in the earth."
The Lord Almighty is with us;
the God of Jacob is our fortress.

Psalm 67

May God be gracious to us and bless us
and make his face shine on us—
so that your ways may be known on earth,
your salvation among all nations.
May the peoples praise you, God;
may all the peoples praise you.
May the nations be glad and sing for joy,
for you rule the peoples with equity
and guide the nations of the earth.
May the peoples praise you, God;
may all the peoples praise you.
The land yields its harvest;
God, our God, blesses us.
May God bless us still,
so that all the ends of the earth will fear him.

Psalm 100

Shout for joy to the Lord, all the earth.
Worship the Lord with gladness;
come before him with joyful songs.
Know that the Lord is God.
It is he who made us, and we are his;
we are his people, the sheep of his pasture.
Enter his gates with thanksgiving
and his courts with praise;
give thanks to him and praise his name.
For the Lord is good and his love endures forever,
his faithfulness continues through all generations.

Psalm 103

Praise the Lord, my soul;
all my inmost being, praise his holy name.
Praise the Lord, my soul,
and forget not all his benefits—
who forgives all your sins
and heals all your diseases,
who redeems your life from the pit
and crowns you with love and compassion,
who satisfies your desires with good things
so that your youth is renewed like the eagle's.
The Lord works righteousness
and justice for all the oppressed.
He made known his ways to Moses,
his deeds to the people of Israel:
The Lord is compassionate and gracious,
slow to anger, abounding in love.
He will not always accuse,
nor will he harbor his anger forever;
he does not treat us as our sins deserve
or repay us according to our iniquities.
For as high as the heavens are above the earth,
so great is his love for those who fear him;
as far as the east is from the west,
so far has he removed our transgressions from us.
As a father has compassion on his children,
so the Lord has compassion on those who fear him;
for he knows how we are formed,

he remembers that we are dust.
The life of mortals is like grass,
they flourish like a flower of the field;
the wind blows over it and it is gone,
and its place remembers it no more.
But from everlasting to everlasting
the Lord's love is with those who fear him,
and his righteousness with their children's children—
with those who keep his covenant
and remember to obey his precepts.
The Lord has established his throne in heaven,
and his kingdom rules over all.
Praise the Lord, you his angels,
you mighty ones who do his bidding,
who obey his word.
Praise the Lord, all his heavenly hosts,
you his servants who do his will.
Praise the Lord, all his works
everywhere in his dominion.
Praise the Lord, my soul.

Psalm 121

I lift up my eyes to the mountains—
where does my help come from?
My help comes from the Lord,
the Maker of heaven and earth.
He will not let your foot slip—
he who watches over you will not slumber;
indeed, he who watches over Israel
will neither slumber nor sleep.
The Lord watches over you—
the Lord is your shade at your right hand;
the sun will not harm you by day,
nor the moon by night.
The Lord will keep you from all harm—
he will watch over your life;
the Lord will watch over your coming and going
both now and forevermore.

Psalm 130

Out of the depths I cry to you, Lord;
Lord, hear my voice.
Let your ears be attentive
to my cry for mercy.
If you, Lord, kept a record of sins,
Lord, who could stand?
But with you there is forgiveness,
so that we can, with reverence, serve you.
I wait for the Lord, my whole being waits,
and in his word I put my hope.
I wait for the Lord
more than watchmen wait for the morning,
more than watchmen wait for the morning.
Israel, put your hope in the Lord,
for with the Lord is unfailing love
and with him is full redemption.
He himself will redeem Israel
from all their sins.

Psalm 131

My heart is not proud, Lord,
my eyes are not haughty;
I do not concern myself with great matters
or things too wonderful for me.
But I have calmed and quieted myself,
I am like a weaned child with its mother;
like a weaned child I am content.
Israel, put your hope in the Lord
both now and forevermore.

Psalm 134

Praise the Lord, all you servants of the Lord
who minister by night in the house of the Lord.
Lift up your hands in the sanctuary
and praise the Lord.
May the Lord bless you from Zion,
he who is the Maker of heaven and earth.

Psalm 150

Praise the Lord.
Praise God in his sanctuary;
praise him in his mighty heavens.
Praise him for his acts of power;
praise him for his surpassing greatness.
Praise him with the sounding of the trumpet,
praise him with the harp and lyre,
praise him with timbrel and dancing,
praise him with the strings and pipe,
praise him with the clash of cymbals,
praise him with resounding cymbals.
Let everything that has breath praise the Lord.
Praise the Lord.

Living the Liturgy

The Eucharistic liturgy, Holy Communion, is the principal service in most Anglican churches Sunday by Sunday, and its focus is on remembering, in sacrament, the presence of the Lord.

> For where two or three gather in my name, there am I with them.
>
> ***Matthew 18:20***

Eucharist is the Greek word for thanksgiving and has its roots in the pastoral meal, the Last Supper, when Jesus blessed bread and wine, shared these with his disciples and said: "this is my body ... this is my blood ... do this in remembrance of me." The Eucharist is an act of union with Christ as he offers himself in sacrifice in bread and wine to the Church, and, in our sacrificial service to others in his name, we become the sacrificed body of Christ to the world. The Eucharist binds us not only with Christ's sacrifice in the past but also to the very throne and Kingdom of God made present, now and for all eternity.

God's presence is not confined within the walls of a sacred building. As a young man working in the city of London, I often attended the lunchtime Eucharist in one of the many restored Wren churches. On one occasion I was near the Central Criminal Court, and after communion I went to a sandwich bar opposite to have a spot of lunch before returning to the office. The café was filled with lawyers, and members of the public who had sat in the gallery of the Old Bailey listening to the proceedings in court that morning, and the talk all around me was about an ongoing sensational murder trial. What greater contrast could there have been? The bread roll and bowl of soup in front of me took on a special significance as I remembered the concluding words of the Eucharist: "Go in peace, to love and serve the Lord." We are not called to be apart from the world but to be Christ's presence, his eyes and ears, his hands and feet, in service to others in his name. Shortly afterwards, I became a Special Constable attached to Bow Street Police Station, and after ordination I trained as a voluntary probation officer whilst serving my title as a curate in Eastbourne, combining my pastoral role with that of public service in the community.

The shape of the liturgy has significance in our understanding of the role of the Church today. The offertory is the offering up of our lives in service to God's will. The prayers of intercession give thanks to God for all that he has done for us in the giving of his Son upon the cross for our salvation, and to remind us that we are called to alleviate the suffering and needs of others in his name, and in partaking of the sacrament, we become the sacrament (the outward and visible sign of an inward and spiritual grace).

> After the Sabbath, at dawn on the first day of the week, Mary Magdalene and the other Mary went to look at the tomb.
>
> There was a violent earthquake, for an angel of the Lord came down from heaven and, going to the tomb, rolled back the stone and sat on it. His appearance was like lightning, and his clothes were white as snow. The guards were so afraid of him that they shook and became like dead men.
>
> The angel said to the women, "Do not be afraid, for I know that you are looking for Jesus, who was crucified. He is not here; he has risen, just as he said. Come and see the place where he lay. Then go quickly and tell his disciples: 'He has risen from the dead and is going ahead of you into Galilee. There you will see him.' Now I have told you."
>
> So the women hurried away from the tomb, afraid yet filled with joy, and ran to tell his disciples. Suddenly Jesus met them. "Greetings," he said. They came to him, clasped his feet and worshipped him. Then Jesus said to them, "Do not be afraid. Go and tell my brothers to go to Galilee; there they will see me."

Then the eleven disciples went to Galilee, to the mountain where Jesus had told them to go. When they saw him, they worshipped him; but some doubted. Then Jesus came to them and said, "All authority in heaven and on earth has been given to me. Therefore go and make disciples of all nations, baptizing them in the name of the Father and of the Son and of the Holy Spirit, and teaching them to obey everything I have commanded you. And surely I am with you always, to the very end of the age."

Matthew 28:1–10, 16–20

Epilogue

In the crypt of St Paul's Cathedral is a memorial to its architect, Sir Christopher Wren:

LECTOR, SI MONUMENTUM
REQUIRIS, CIRCUMSPICE
(Reader, if you seek his monument—look around you.)

If you seek God, look within, and there you will surely find him. If you seek evidence of his handiwork, look around you and you will find evidence of his presence in every act of unselfish love and commitment to the wellbeing of others, for God is love, and love is of God.

> Whoever does not love does not know God, because God is love. This is how God showed his love among us: He sent his one and only Son into the world that we might live through him. This is love: not that we loved God, but that he loved us and sent his Son as an atoning sacrifice for our sins.
>
> ***1 John 4:8-10***

EU GPSR Authorized Representative:

LOGOS EUROPE, 9 rue Nicolas Poussin, 17000 La Rochelle, France

contact@logoseurope.eu

www.ingramcontent.com/pod-product-compliance
Lightning Source LLC
LaVergne TN
LVHW020939090426
835512LV00020B/3436